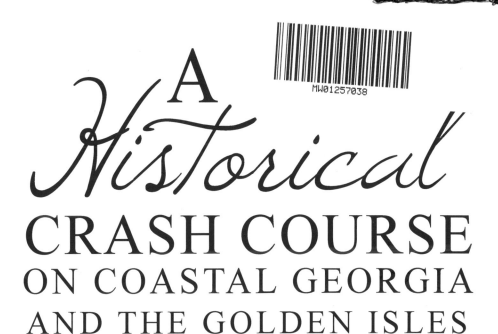

A Historical
CRASH COURSE
ON COASTAL GEORGIA
AND THE GOLDEN ISLES
as told by Buddy Sullivan

BY LARRY HOBBS
Staff writer —The Brunswick News

THE BRUNSWICK
NEWS

Introduction

*"It's all now you see. Yesterday won't be over until tomorrow
and tomorrow began ten thousand years ago."*
— *William Faulkner, Intruder in the Dust*

The brilliant Southern writer was well-known for blending the past and present until the two concepts appeared indistinguishable. Yeah, Faulkner was out there all right.

But such continuity does not appear quite so crazy here in the Golden Isles and along the rest of the Georgia Coast, where a long and rich history reaches out to us daily. The past is present virtually everywhere you look around here. In some areas along this beautiful coast, folks might pass three or four historic landmarks just dropping the kids off at school or keeping a doctor's appointment. Streets, neighborhoods and institutions bear the names of those who plied these waters and trod this land before us. National and state historic parks abound, preserving for posterity yet another stately plantation, Spartan fortification or the site of some monumental conflagration.

Yet these tangible reminders are but one dimension of our connection to the region's storied past. Their presence among us is palpable; their imprint is enduring, ageless.

Untold generations have been reinventing these shores, and their place among them, since the first Europeans arrived nearly 500 years ago. Native Americans reaped the bounty of Coastal Georgia's natural resources on both land and sea for eons before that.

The myriad scope of human endeavor that has transpired here is staggering: Indian settlements, Spanish missions, British colonies,

Larry Hobbs

Antebellum plantations, and timber mills; commerce aboard oceangoing tall ships, river rafts, railroads, and trade routes; great struggles of revolution and independence, war and peace, bondage and freedom.

I hold an abiding love and appreciation for everything to do with history, particularly American history. And for that reason, I feel blessed to live on St. Simons Island, which is pretty much the geographical heart of Coastal Georgia. On a typical bicycle ride from one end of the island to the other, I may encounter historical sites and markers that document all of the above-mentioned periods.

I learn something new just about every time I venture out, not to mention all the great history waiting to be absorbed on the mainland as well as up and down the coast. Someday I would like to sort it all out, I have said to myself more than once.

But my job as a reporter with The Brunswick News keeps me pretty busy; you know, all that writing about the here and now.

Buddy Sullivan started out as a newspaperman himself, just up the road from here in Darien, Ga. Mr. Sullivan ("Please, call me Buddy," he always says) is now a highly-regarded historian. He is a recognized authority, in fact, on the ever-fascinating and always relevant history of Coastal Georgia. Buddy (http://www.buddysullivan.com) is the author of some 25 books on the subject, and has earned a slew of awards and accolades, including the Lilla M. Hawes Award for outstanding book on Georgia history (2001) and the National History Award Medal from the Daughters of the American Revolution.

He also served on the Georgia Historical Society's board of curators for 11 years, and was Director of the Sapelo Island National Estuarine Research Reserve from 1993 to 2013. He presently is the Senior Historian of the Coastal Georgia Historical Society (https://www.coastalgeorgiahistory.org).

He is much in demand as a speaker and lecturer on the topic. One of

Buddy's more popular events is the annual six-week lecture series he presents each year at the St. Simons Lighthouse Museum, sponsored by the Coastal Georgia Historical Society. This year I proposed to my editor, Mike Hall, that I sit in on Buddy's lecture series and write about it for The News.

The result was a series of six articles in The News, appearing on successive Sundays from January 22-February 26, 2017. The other result was this little book. It is a literal crash course on Coastal Georgia history, as told by Buddy Sullivan. It covers everything from this singularly-distinct coast's geological formation up to its prominent American role in the 20th Century.

It is by no means a complete history, nor is it intended to be. What it does do is give a good chronological overview of Coastal Georgia history. And what a captivating story that is. This region has been the stage for centuries of human drama, covering triumph and tragedy, heartbreak and joy, transgression and redemption. The tale is set in one of the most unique and enduring ecosystems on earth, one that its narrator knows by heart.

But the best accolade I can offer for this book is that it comes to you with Buddy's endorsement. He noted early on that my articles were entertaining, detailed and factual. By week four of the lecture series it was not too much of a stretch to tell my publisher it was all Buddy's idea to make a book out of it. A true Southern gentleman, Buddy has offered guidance and resources from the start.

The first six chapters are basically a slightly-edited reprint of The News articles, done so with Publisher Buff Levy's blessing. I am most grateful to him for this and so much more.

I wrote two additional chapters just for this book. One is on the history of women on the Georgia Coast and the other touches on the African American experience here. While neither is neglected from the overall story, some very good details were necessarily left out because of space and the overall flow of the narrative.

I hope y'all enjoy reading this half as much as I enjoyed writing it.

Peace — Larry Hobbs, April 19, 2017

Table of Contents

Part 1: Unique Ecosystem is the Heart of Coastal Georgia

To hear Buddy Sullivan tell it, the history of the Golden Isles begins 25,000 years ago at the tail end of the last Ice Age, the one scientists call the Pleistocene.

And so that is where it all starts when Buddy Sullivan tells it each year at the St. Simons Island Lighthouse Museum under the sponsorship of the Coastal Georgia Historical Society. For more than 20 years now, this well-versed local historian has a kept a rendezvous with a faithful audience of folks clamoring to learn more about this unique region's long and storied past.

Since 1995, Sullivan has returned each balmy winter to present his six-week lectures series in the museum's A.W. Jones Heritage Center, an event that has become as predictable as the tides that dictate the rhythms of life along the Georgia Coast. The Brunswick News reserved a seat for the 2017 series, joining about 100 or so others who turned out to hear Buddy Sullivan tell it.

From the region's basic formation in that distant Pleistocene era, things moved quickly during that action-packed first lecture. In the course of the next two hours, Sullivan expounded on Native American recycling practices, foolhardy conquistadors, martyred Jesuit priests, and secret ruins. Heck, the attendees

Hazzard's Ballast Island near Sapelo Sound

didn't even hear a thing about the well-known tales of Fort Frederica and British Gen. James Oglethorpe until the second lecture.

Sullivan's geography lesson on the opening day included the vivid and heartfelt description of a "ballast island" in McIntosh County. There a boy once washed down Vienna sausages with natural well water while fishing the day away.

That is among of the many personal anecdotes that Sullivan might sprinkle into his lectures. Newcomers to the series learn quickly that this classroom's professor comes by his love of the subject matter naturally. The Darien native was born to it. This insight became apparent in the series' opening round, after the Georgia coast's primary barrier islands formed during that Ice Age.

Sullivan spoke lovingly of the lush and prolific tidal system that evolved between those islands and the mainland — the largest and most unique salt marsh system on the entire Atlantic coast.

"I grew up on the marsh," said Sullivan, author of more than 20 books on Coastal Georgia history. "Probably the first smell I knew in my existence was the salt marsh. And I've loved it ever since. You become acculturated to the marsh. It's part of who you are and where you've been and where you came from. So the marshes are very important."

He touched on the importance of the estuaries, where Atlantic saltwater meets freshwater at rivers like the Altamaha and the Satilla. Through the course of migration and breeding, an abundance of marine life courses from still waters into swelling oceans through the open sounds between each of these barrier islands. The dry land is characterized by dense "maritime forests," consisting of live oaks, Longleaf pine, red cedar and a thick underbrush of palmetto and myrtle.

The spongy soil beneath has provided fertile farm land since the Guale Indians first settled on the barrier islands some 6,000 years ago, Sullivan said. Archaeologists have gleaned much about these first inhabitants to the Golden Isles by digging through the "shell rings" that marked their settlements. They lived in walled villages, which they buttressed with oyster shells and other refuse from their seafood diets. There is one on Sapelo Island nearly 300 feet across that might have stood 25 feet high in its heyday 4,000 years ago; a smaller "shell ring" can be found at Cannon's Point on St. Simons Island.

The crops those native Americans were farming when Europeans arrived to the Georgia Coast in the early 1,500s included produce that would be recognizable in a grocery store today, from squash and peas to corn and cantaloupe, Sullivan said.

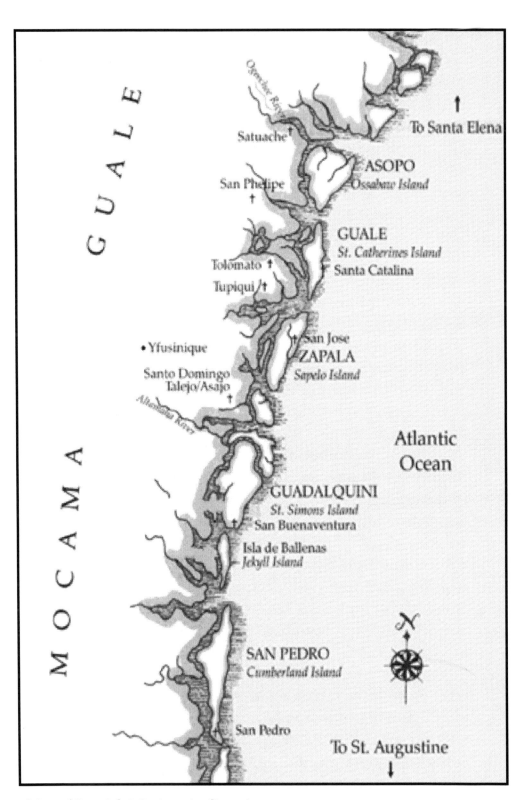

Map of Spanish Missions in Georgia

As Sullivan put it to his audience: The coast's teeming waters, and the bountiful lands they surround, provide an attraction for settlement that has prevailed throughout human habitation here. "You should never go hungry on the Georgia Coast," Sullivan said. "There is plenty of game, fish, shrimp, crabs and oysters. A lot of the things we go into Publix (supermarket) and buy today were grown by the native Americans right here."

Even still, the first settlers on the Georgia Coast found the going rough. With the King of Spain's seal of approval, Lucas Vázquez de Ayllón established in 1526 a short-lived settlement of about 500 soldiers, African slaves, settlers and Jesuits — probably somewhere near Sapelo Sound. The exact location of the settlement of San Miguel de Guadalupe has yet to be found, but we know it existed based on the Spaniards' meticulous record-keeping.

Hundreds died of disease and starvation, and the rest returned home after barely two years. Sullivan suspects the settlement's location will one day be revealed, if through nothing else the burial ground of those who perished in the unfamiliar and inhospitable climate.

"Archaeologists have been diligently searching for the location," Sullivan said. "Nobody's found anything yet. I suspect one day somebody will."

Less elusive are the Spanish missions that followed beginning in the 1570s. These included Santo Domingo near Fort King George in Darien, San Buenos Ventura on the south end of St. Simons Island and San Pedro on Cumberland Island. Due to pressures from unfriendly natives, Santo Domingo relocated to St. Simons Island's north end — probably near Cannon's Point — and was renamed Asajo in 1661.

Most impressive of all is Santa Catalina, which was discovered a mere 35 years ago on St. Catherine's

Island by the archaeologist David Hearst Thomas. The find has netted a treasure trove of native and Spanish artifacts, including pewter ware, ceramics and religious medallions — much of which is now held at Fernbank Museum of Natural History in Atlanta.

But don't expect to visit the site of the settlement on St. Catherine's. Sullivan is among the tight-lipped circle of folks who know its location, which remains a guarded secret to thwart pillagers.

"I'm probably one of the few people who knows where it is," Sullivan said. "Why do they keep it a secret? Artifact hunters. Looters."

Two of the priests at Santa Catalina were among five murdered at missions along the Georgia coast during a 1597 native uprising. The Roman Catholic Diocese of Savannah consecrated the grounds of Santa Catalina in 1985, and has submitted the five slain priests to the Vatican for martyrdom and eventual sainthood, Sullivan said.

"It takes a great deal of time for the process of sainthood," Sullivan said. "But I hope it comes to pass. I really do."

This era of local history was not part of the curriculum back when Sullivan was a schoolboy growing up in Darien. Much of it was simply unknown until later in the 20th Century. It took the digging of archaeologists like Thomas and the delving of historians like author Paul Hoffman to uncover it. Hoffman was the man who actually went to Spain and researched 500-year-old records to discover the existence of San Miguel de Guadalupe.

"In eighth grade Georgia History, the first day of class was a little bit about Indians and a bit on Spanish missions," he said. "And the next day of class Oglethorpe was landing to found Savannah and the Georgia colony. Now we're discovering this rich history of more than 200 years before Oglethorpe came."

Oglethorpe's arrival would open the seas to regular trade between Old World and New — creating less vintage geological formations such as Hazards Island where Sullivan fished a child. The large ballast rocks that helped empty-hulled ships navigate the Atlantic were dumped to make room for the return trip with badly-needed timber and other plentiful commodities obtained here in the Americas.

And before the modern paper mills came and drained the natural artesian wells around here, there was plenty of fresh water to drink once you reached the island, Sullivan recalled.

"You could sit right there on the rocks and there was even a freshwater well," he said. "You could have your Vienna sausages and your saltines and fish till your heart's content and have plenty of water.

"These marshes touch our lives in some way or another in virtually everything we do," he added.

Part 2: The story of Robert Jenkins' ear and other tales

Just about everybody in these parts has heard at least something about The War of Jenkins' Ear, but scarce few know anything at all about Robert Jenkins' actual ear.

Coastal Georgia historian Buddy Sullivan remedied this historical omission during the second session of his lecture series. And he peppered his talk with plenty of similarly elusive local tidbits, providing the history behind the history of Coastal Georgia's storied past.

For instance, the locally-famous 1742 Battle of Bloody Marsh on St. Simons Island was not really all that bloody, Sullivan explained. And it was not nearly as significant in squashing Spanish designs on possession of Georgia territory as was a brutish ambush that took place earlier that day near present-day Oglethorpe Point Elementary School.

Also, Sullivan shed light on a prominent member of McIntosh County's founding family, a man who earned both fame and infamy during the American Revolution.

And then there is Brunswick. The city we know today is named for German royalty and has retained Old World English refinement in street names like Prince and (King) George. But its earliest incarnation was as a

James Edward Oglethorpe, founder of Georgia

tobacco farm called Plug Point.

"It was the first known tobacco farm in Georgia," Sullivan told his audience.

Georgia itself began as private enterprise with lofty ideals, Sullivan noted. British Gen. James Oglethorpe founded the colony as a means of easing the misery of those languishing their lives away in England's crowded debtors' prisons. These debtors instead would be given the opportunity to carve out a new life in a strange land rather than suffer in a decrepit prison.

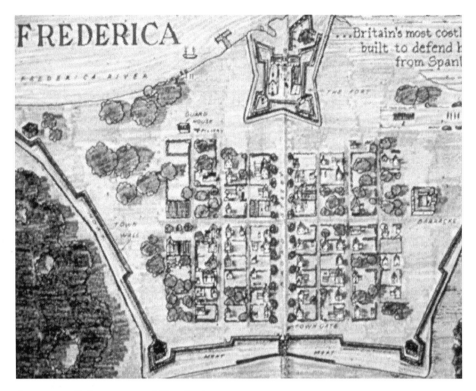

Layout of the town of Frederica

Oglethorpe was influenced considerably in this endeavor by his association with the theologian brothers, Charles and John Wesley, Anglicans who stayed briefly in Georgia and would go on to lay the foundations of the Methodist Church.

"Georgia really became a philanthropic endeavor," Sullivan explained. "They had begun to look at ways to deal with debtors. If you accumulated debts, you went to prison. And they couldn't pay their debts if they were in prison."

The original colony got its direction from a private board of trustees, of which Oglethorpe was a member. It was the last of Britain's 13 colonies to be established on the North American Continent. But the whole debtor relief idea never really caught on, Sullivan said.

Scottish Highlanders helped save St. Simons

"Very few debtors ever came to Georgia, even though this is the reason Georgia was established," Sullivan said. "History has shown that only a handful of debtors ever came over."

But the colony was still infused with high ideals. For one, Georgia originally banned slavery. Also, hard liquor was not tolerated — colonists could quench their thirst for alcohol with beer and wine only. Additionally, lawyers were not welcome. What the colonists did have was a tough and competent leader in Oglethorpe.

"Oglethorpe was the key to the whole thing, the glue that held it together," Sullivan said. "I can't emphasize enough how crucial Oglethorpe was to the colony of Georgia. He made it clear: If you don't work, you don't eat. He had a lot of energy and passion. A lot of them wanted to quit but Oglethorpe held it together. He said, 'We are going to make this work without slavery and without gin and rum.'"

The new colony also boasted almost complete religious freedom. Folks of the Jewish faith were encouraged to settle here. So too were the followers of differing protestant teachings, from the German Salzburgers to the Dutch Reform Church to the Presbyterian Scottish Highlanders. It seems everyone was welcome — except the Catholics. Catholics were initially banned from the colony.

This ban was largely a product of Britain's long-standing feud with Spain, which was a nation of Catholics. The two nations' mutual animosity quickly took root overseas, where it festered within the greed for empire and power in the New World. By the 18th Century, Spain held a tenuous foothold in Florida while the British occupied everything to the north. Britain's newest colony was considered disputed territory and a point of contention by the Spanish.

Britain's first settlement in Georgia was Fort King George, established in 1721 near present day Darien. Fort Frederica came along in 1736, built along the Frederica River the central area of St. Simons Island's west side. The settlement consisted of a heavily-fortified military installation, secured by a wall and a moat. It was surrounded by a town of wide-ranging tradesmen, from candle makers to blacksmiths to animal husbandry.

The fort's soldiers included the sturdy Scottish Highlanders, renowned at the time for a deadly-efficient style of guerrilla warfare.

"Heaven forbid you make fun of the kilts they wore with their uniforms, because they were fierce warriors," Sullivan said. "Fort Frederica was the most ambitious military fortification of its time in North America. It was a very compact, self-sufficient town, conceived to support the military installation."

All of which brings us to The War of Jenkins' Ear.

"It's a very unusual name for a war, isn't it?" Sullivan quipped.

The war that forever settled any claims Spain eyed north of Florida had as its origins an incident in 1729 in the West Indies. A Spanish military captain boarded the merchant ship of British sea trader and a suspected smuggler named Robert Jenkins. The captain demanded to see Jenkins' papers. Jenkins refused. The captain grew irate. Very irate.

"He lost his temper, cut Jenkins' ear off and stormed off," Sullivan said. "Jenkins put the ear in a jar of brine, went on to London and said, 'Here's my ear. A Spanish captain cut if off and I did nothing to provoke him.'"

Oglethorpe went on the offensive in 1740, launching a failed attack on St. Augustine that ended when British troops could not dislodge the Spanish from Fort Mose. Two years later, the Spanish came calling on St. Simons Island, bringing with them some 3,000 troops loaded onto about 40 ships.

The Spanish landed on the south end of St. Simons Island in early July of 1742. A couple of days later a reconnaissance force of about 250 Spanish troops set out to scout Fort Frederica. Instead, the Spanish stumbled into an ambush on July 7 at Gully Hole Creek just outside the town of Frederica. Highlanders, soldiers and natives commanded by Oglethorpe fired away with devastating results on the Spanish, who left behind 36 dead or captured as they fled in panic.

By the time the legendary Battle of Bloody Marsh unfolded farther south on St. Simons Island later that day, Spanish commanders apparently were looking for any excuse to abandon their expedition. After a comparatively benign exchange of gunfire, the Spanish boarded their ships and returned to Florida with tales of being woefully undermanned for the mission.

"I know we've all heard of Bloody Marsh, but the real battle was Gully Hole Creek," Sullivan said.

"It was much more important than what happened at Bloody Marsh. The Spanish were sounds defeated at Gully Hole Creek. They reported being vastly outnumbered. If they had only done their homework, it was the British who were greatly outnumbered."

Others from Coastal Georgia's distant past whose names still ring familiar today include Capt. Raymond Demere and Lachlan McIntosh. Capt. Demere was placed in charge of Fort Frederica by Oglethorpe himself. However, Demere might cringe at today's pronunciation of the St. Simons Island thoroughfare that bears his name.

"He became a large property owner and a very important person in Georgia," Sullivan said. "But he pronounced his name, 'Dem-e-ray,' and now we call it 'Dem-ry.'"

McIntosh was the son of John Mohr McIntosh, an early settler of New Inverness, founded by the Highlanders in 1736, and which later became Darien. The younger McIntosh was a leader in Georgia's efforts during the American Revolution, and a hot-headed one at that. He became embroiled in a political dispute with Georgia politician Button Gwinnett, a signer of the Declaration of Independence and the namesake of Gwinnett County. Both men were adamant that the dispute could be settled only at 12 paces with pistols.

"Gwinnett and McIntosh fired pistols at each other," Sullivan said. "Both were shot, and Gwinnett's wounds proved to be
fatal."

Brunswick's first settler was Captain Mark Carr, an English officer who served under Oglethorpe. He started his Plug Point tobacco farm in 1738 on 1,000 acres granted to him in Brunswick's south end as reward for his service to the crown. The town that followed is named for the duchy of King George III's ancestral home in Germany. Most American cities discarded the English street names and other geographic references to Britain in the wake of the Revolutionary War. Not Brunswick. Union Street, for example, is named for the "union of England and Scotland," Sullivan said.

"Many towns after independence changed names to dissolve their ties to England," Sullivan said. "But Brunswick kept them. I'm glad they kept it. It gives Brunswick a lot of its character."

Part 3: Plantation Intrigue, Old Ironsides in the Antebellum

A six-week melodramatic television miniseries would be a more fitting forum than a newspaper for sorting out the intrigues of antebellum-era plantation families, their loves and their losses in the Golden Isles.

And y'all can bet the ratings for that miniseries would hang on the improbable marriage of a slave-holding St. Simons Island plantation scion to an abolitionist celebrity actress. A plot of such far-fetched schlock would fly these days only on the Oxygen or Lifetime networks, right?

That, or in the capable hands of Buddy Sullivan. The popular Coastal Georgia historian presented the facts with a touch of fancy, dishing on the real-life and short-lived marriage of Pierce M. Butler to Fanny Kemble in 1834. In the third installment of his annual six-week lecture series at the St. Simons Lighthouse Museum, Sullivan weaved this story seamlessly into the thick web of Hamiltons and Spaldings and Coupers and Butlers — the families that reigned locally in the plantation days.

But the rich history that unfolded here on the Georgia Coast between the end of the Revolutionary War (1783) and the beginning of the Civil War (1861) could

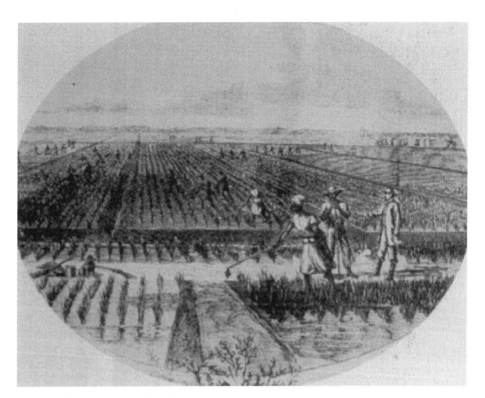

Rice cultivation in the Altamaha delta

hardly be contained only by those rich and privileged classes. There was the timber boom on Gascoigne Bluff and Cannon's Point, launched by a shipbuilder's desire to shore up the fledgling United States Navy in the decades after independence.

The live oaks that had grown untouched for centuries on St. Simons Island were ideal for Joshua Humphries' designs for sturdy seagoing war ships. The trees' massive, curling limbs were particularly prized as perfectly configured for the massive timbers that formed the stout framework of these ships of war.

This era between 1790 and the early 1800s started a wave of immigration to the area from Boston and parts north — timber cutters and shipbuilders who followed Humphries to St. Simons Island.

"St. Simons really became an important center,"

Butler's Island rice mill chimney

Sullivan said. "The Georgia live oak was recognized as highly desirable for ship building. And it thrived in the porous soils and salt air here. Humphries wanted to design ships that would out-class anything in the world."

Humphries got his wish, most famously with the construction of the USS Constitution, the 44-gun frigate that time and again bested the best the vaunted British Navy sent against it in the War of 1812. So sturdy were the ship's oaken hulls that the hapless Brits suspected the materials were forged rather than felled.

"The most famous of these ships was the USS Constitution, also known as?" Sullivan said, engaging his audience.

"Old Ironsides," audience members responded in unison.

Restored slave cabin at Hamilton plantation

"It was so durable that some of the British sailors said the cannonballs bounced off the ship and that's how it got its nickname," the Darien native said. "If that actually happened — and I doubt it did — that speaks to the durability of St. Simons live oak."

Sprawling plantations of the antebellum period also were coming into their own in this time. If cotton was king in the rest of the South, rice reigned in Coastal Georgia. With rivers like the Altamaha and the Ogeechee flowing into sweeping tidal estuaries, the conditions were prime for cultivating rice.

Sometimes the facts need no embellishment. Sometimes history is just plain ugly without it. Georgia founder James Oglethorpe's lofty ambitions of establishing a colony free of slavery had long since been forgotten by this time.

John Couper of Cannon's Point

"The rice was planted by slaves, of course," Sullivan said. "This was all based on slave labor. Rice plantations required a high degree of labor. They were the most labor intensive of all the plantations in the south. Rice plantations always had the largest slave populations."

Planter Pierce Butler alone owned 600 slaves to work his 1,500-acre plantation on Butler Island on the McIntosh County side of the Altamaha River. There were four "slave settlements" scattered about the plantation. In 1859, the plantation

Map of St. Simon's plantations

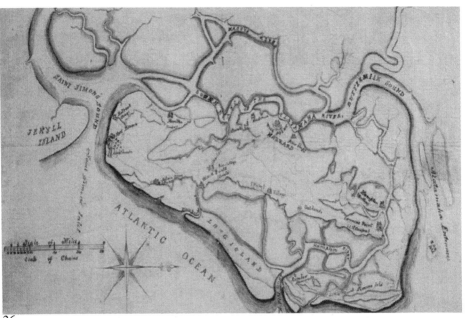

Fanny Kemble, wife of Pierce M. Butler

produced 1.6 million pounds of white rice for the commercial market, Sullivan said. Rice plantations lined both sides of the Altamaha, along Glynn and McIntosh counties. In the era leading up to the Civil War, South Carolina and Georgia produced 96 percent of the world's marketable rice, Sullivan said.

"Rice was a minor crop overall in the South, but here it was the No. 1 crop," Sullivan said.

The fields were flooded four times during the annual planting season. Planters employed a system of wooden flood gates and the natural flow of incoming fresh river water on the outgoing tides. The fields also were drained on the outgoing tides. Saltwater encroachment from incoming tides would destroy the crops.

Like the labor force, this system of rice cultivation the wealthy planters used also was taken from Africa.

"They adopted techniques that had been used by Africans in West Africa," Sullivan said. "These techniques involved a system of planting rice on the tidal-flow system of agriculture. They used the natural river system. They used the ecosystem to work for them. This was a very technologically-advanced system for the time."

The chimney of a steam-powered rice mill on Butler's Island remains visible today for motorists approaching Darien on U.S. Highway 17.

Maj. Pierce Butler also ran Hampton Plantation on St. Simons Island, growing the highly-favored Sea Island cotton, a strand developed in the West Indies and used in such luxury textiles as lace and fine curtains.

James Hamilton established the Hamilton Plantation on Gascoigne Bluff. His friend and fellow Scotsman John Couper established his plantation at Cannon's Point. James Spalding established the Orange Hall/Retreat Plantation on the southern end of St. Simons Island.

Couper is the most remarkable of these founding planters, in Sullivan's opinion. The former apprentice from Savannah and supporter of the Revolution bought the Cannon's Point property in 17aa93 and built the plantation up from there. John and wife Rebecca's dinner parties and gatherings at their elegant estate were known throughout the new nation.

"He was very innovative and very resourceful and used the ecosystem to further his estate," Sullivan said. "He was one of the most interesting of all the planters. And they loved to entertain and hold parties. It was a social mecca."

He also provided the land for St. Simons Island's first lighthouse and recruited James Gould from New England to build it. It was completed in 1811 (and torn down in the Civil War by retreating Confederates). The Gould's Inlet namesake liked his finished product so much he became its first lighthouse keeper.

The offspring of the original plantation founders spawned many more stories, all which Sullivan captured in detail through his lecture.

And all of these island plantations, of course, depended on the human toil of slave labor. Which brings us back to the matrimony of Pierce M. Butler and

Fanny Kemble. Butler was the grandson of Maj. Butler, and also something of a snowbird. He inherited the St. Simons Island and Butler's Island plantations, but preferred living in his birthplace, Philadelphia, Penn.

That is where he met and fell in love with Frances Anne (Fanny) Kemble, a beloved Shakespearian actress from England who was on tour there in 1832. The affection, apparently, was mutual. Kemble was an intelligent woman, not known for keeping her opinions to herself; Butler had inherited hundreds of slaves.

"She had to have known her husband was the largest slave holder in Georgia," Sullivan said. "And she was a very gifted writer and a leading abolitionist."

After years of back-and-forth between the two, Fanny convinced Butler to let her visit the family plantations in Dec. of 1838. She stayed but four months.

In that time, however, her visits to the slave quarters and her observations of the deprivations resulted in a book, Journal of a Residence of a Georgian Plantation, 1838-1839. One historian described the book as the "most detailed look at plantation slavery ever recorded by a white northern abolitionist."

They were divorced in 1839. "Her husband was just livid," Sullivan said.

In addition to her stark observations of slave conditions, Fanny wrote lovingly about Coastal Georgia's flora and fauna.

"She detailed the slavery, of course" Sullivan said. "But the beauty of the Georgia coast was not lost on her."

Part 4: Civil War comes to the Golden Isles, Darien burns

ong before Gen. Sherman's scorched earth policy made Georgia howl all the way from Atlanta to Savannah, the Union Army made an example of defenseless Darien by plundering it and burning it to the ground.

Perhaps no one was more outraged by this pitiless assault on the secluded coastal hamlet than Col. Robert Gould Shaw, the man who ordered his 54th Massachusetts regiment of free blacks to take part in the senseless debacle on June 11, 1863. Appalled that his troops would be used for such an inglorious purpose, Col. Shaw participated in the burning of Darien only under the threat of court martial from his commanding officer, Sullivan noted.

Sullivan says the Boston abolitionist's conflicted emotions are accurately depicted in "Glory," the 1989 Academy Award-winning movie that chronicles the fighting determination of black troops to prove their worth during the Civil War.

"Actually, Shaw did it under duress," Sullivan said. "Shaw protested the burning of the town because he felt like this was taking war to innocent civilians."

The sacking of Darien seared a hollow gash through the centuries-old history of Sullivan's home town, and

Gen. Wiliam T. Sherman

Col. Robert G. Shaw of the 54th
Massachusetts

stands out as one of the wars more egregious atroci-
ties committed against the civilian populace. Some 18
months later, Gen. William Tecumseh Sherman would
take the strategically vital port of Savannah without
firing so much as a shot within the city limits, Sullivan
said. By this time, white Southerners had long since
retreated from St. Simons Island, Jekyll Island, Brunswick and the rest of the Golden Isles — escaping the
vise grip of Union advances from both land and sea.

The era of burgeoning rice plantations along the
tributary rivers and sprawling cotton estates on the
islands ended for one small segment of the population.
And the war marked the beginning of freedom and the
end of servitude and bondage for a much larger segment of the population.

Most people today associate the Civil War's end with
the somber meeting of Confederate Gen. Robert E. Lee
and Union Gen. Ulysses S. Grant at Appomattox Courthouse in Virginia on April 9, 1865. But here in Coastal
Georgia, the issue was pretty much settled in December

...rman famously made a Christmas
...nah to President Lincoln.
...astal Georgia was concerned, when
...Savannah the war ended," Sullivan said.
...id many folks today might be surprised
...Georgians never wanted the war to start
...place. Slave holders and large landown-
ers c... ...sed only fraction of the state's population.
Those in the majority were not altogether gung-ho
about fighting a war to protect the proprietary interests
of the few. Prior to Georgia's decision to secede from
the Union on Jan. 19 of 1861, a statewide trial referendum passed only through the political machinations of
the land-rich elite, Sullivan said.

"That referendum on secession barely passed," Sullivan said. "One of the things you have to remember is
a very small amount of Georgians owned slaves, less
than 10 percent. So it was not an overwhelmingly popular idea."

And even some of the plantation lords hereabouts
were not too thrilled about going to war. Most notable
among them was Thomas Spalding, the Sapelo Island
planter who employed progressive agricultural meth-
ods and was considered humane in the treatment of his
slaves, Sullivan said.

Spalding was a strong proponent of building struc-
tures with tabby, the cement made with crushed oyster
shells, sand and other readily available local
ingredients. The family's Ashantilly home near Darien
and its plantation home on Sapelo Island, both built in
the Palladium architectural style, stand today as examples of Spalding's use of tabby.

He implemented such advanced agricultural meth-
ods as crop rotation and the adequate planting of non-
commercial crops to sustain the plantation. In addition

Thomas Spalding's Sapelo Island plantation house

to rice and Sea Island cotton, Spalding revolutionized sugar cane farming, including the construction of a tabby sugar cane mill.

Although he owned more than 350 slaves, Spalding abhorred the institution nonetheless. He organized the workloads in a manner that provided slaves with free time, and predicted the practice of slavery would cease within a generation. Although he died before the start of the war, Spalding had voiced his position on the question of secession, Sullivan said.

"He detested slavery," Sullivan said. "He saw it as a necessary evil. He predicted slavery would end anyway and therefore he opposed secession."

In the years leading up to the Civil War, Brunswick and Darien jockeyed for second fiddle to Savannah along the Georgia Coast. Darien had the early advantage, with the Altamaha River reaching the sea at Darien's shores. Before the railroads, cotton and other

Darien waterfront tabby ruins from 1800s

trade goods made it in and out the state's interior via raft on rivers like the Altamaha.

There was even a prestigious Bank of Darien, which was a major financial institution with branches state-wide in the early to mid-19th century.

"Darien was a major port," Sullivan said. "The Altamaha was the main conveyor belt for cotton. From the antebellum capital of Milledgeville and other central points in the state, Darien was the logical choice."

Albeit navigating into the open Atlantic through Darien's Doboy Sound has always required a skilled skipper, Sullivan said. Brunswick, on the other hand, had an ideal harbor. But it had no river to connect it with inland commerce.

"Brunswick never had the benefit of a freshwater river system," Sullivan said. "The paradox is, Brunswick had one of the best natural harbors in the U.S."

Brunswick's answer was the Brunswick-Altamaha Ca-

Remains of Brunswick-Altamaha Canal

nal, a 12-mile manmade waterway that would connect the
Port of Brunswick with that vital river system. The project
got underway in 1836, stalling and sputtering its way to
completion over the next 18 years. The project used slaves
contracted from local plantations, as well as Irish immi-
grant labor.

"And that didn't work so well," Sullivan said.

By its completion in 1854, the project had procrastinat-
ed itself into obsolescence. "It was too late!" Sullivan said.
"Why? That's right, the railroads came along. And Darien
didn't have a railroad. So by the time the Civil War came
around (in 1861), Brunswick and Darien were minor sea-
ports, compared to Savannah and Charleston."

Also, by the time the Civil War came around St. Simons
Island apparently was not worth fighting for. The only fire-
works preceding Union occupation in March of 1862 came
from retreating Confederates, who blew up the 104-foot
lighthouse so the advancing Yankees could not use it.

By that point, most civilians had long since abandoned
St. Simons Island, Jekyll Island and Brunswick. Likewise,
Darien was a virtual ghost town when Col. Shaw's 54th

Massachusetts entered the city along with Col. James Montgomery's 2nd South Carolina Volunteers, comprised of freed slaves. Col. Montgomery had overall command of the operation on that late afternoon.

After encouraging the men to plunder the town of everything from livestock to furniture to silverware, Montgomery instructed Shaw to order his men to put the town to the torch. Shaw had personally taken part in mustering and training the 54th. He found Montgomery's order unbearably demeaning and immoral.

"This created one of the great controversies of the entire war," Sullivan said. "There was no military value to the town; strategically it was unimportant. But the Union commanders wanted to loot the town and then burn it to set an example to the rest of the South.

"Shaw protested, as shown in the very well done movie, 'Glory,'" he added. "Shaw said, 'Why burn the town? There's nobody shooting at us.' They burned people's homes, churches, schools, and the courthouse. That's why we have no records today."

By contrast, Sullivan said there was a sound military objective behind the blazing statewide swath of destruction a year later that made Gen. Sherman famous. Or infamous, depending on which side of the Mason/Dixon line a person leans.

"I grew up and was raised in Coastal Georgia," Sullivan said. "As long as I could remember I was told, 'This man is terrible.' But as I grew older and began to mature in my research, I came to realize he was a military genius. Sherman said, 'War is hell,' and it is. He wanted to destroy the Southern infrastructure and do everything he could to bring an end to the Civil War."

Part 5: Tall Pines Led Coastal Ga. Rebound from Civil War

In the years following the Civil War, old times were more or less forgotten along the Georgia Coast and in the Golden Isles.

With the region spared the ravages that waylaid much of the Deep South during four years of bitter and savage fighting, Coastal Georgians looked away to the inland expanse of tall sturdy pine forest. Within a decade of war's end in 1865, the region began emerging as the leading provider of lumber to a growing nation and the world at large, Sullivan said. As their ancestors had done for centuries before them, post-war Georgians along the coast turned to the land to provide the way.

"This goes back to the ecological circumstances of the area that we have talked about since week one," Sullivan said during the fifth lecture in the series. "The ecology of that region was such that it held some of the most harvestable pine timber, not just in America, but in the entire world. Everything was just chaos in the South. In coastal Georgia, though, the economy was able to recover more quickly than you would see in other parts of the South. A good bit of this was predicated on the timber industry."

Timber cutting made the Coastal Georgia economy thrive

The decades between the Civil War and the dawn of the 20th Century stood witness to an unprecedented era of growth, expansion and transformation for the Golden Isles and the greater coast. That boom was not rooted in timber alone. The area also was a worldwide market for "naval stores" — an anachronistic term for all things pine sap, from turpentine to varnish to shoe polish. The lumber and other pine products were needed by a restless nation, which pushed ever westward as the Transcontinental Railway filled in the space from sea to shining sea.

This expansion made wealthy titans of men like Rockefeller and Vanderbilt and Pulitzer. These tycoons would literally buy Jekyll Island and make it a balmy wintertime retreat of the nation's most rich and powerful. St. Simons Island also dipped its toe in the beachside tourism industry of the era. And Brunswick, finally, began to flourish as a shipping port after gener-

St. Simons Mills at Gascoigne Bluff, late 1800s

ations of bold starts and ill-timed setbacks.

Along coastal Glynn and McIntosh counties Antebellum plantations gave way to bustling timber mills and turpentine distilleries.

So folks in the Golden Isles largely shrugged off the Southern stigma of Reconstruction, rolled up their sleeves and went to work. Joining them was a new kind of American citizen — the freedmen. Former slaves once bound to coastal cotton and rice plantations returned of their own free will to St. Simons Island, Sapelo Island and surrounding environs to carve new paths to freedom. Their ability to pursue life, liberty and happiness by working in the timber industry contributed significantly to the local economy's rebound, Sullivan said.

"There were quite a number of free slaves who came back to the Sea Islands," Sullivan said. "This was understandable because it was all they knew. They were able to come back, get work and acquire small savings and actually get loans. The timber industry is really what led many of the free people in Coastal Georgia to

Brunswick's port prospered with naval stores

buy property and own homes."

Planter Pierce Butler even managed to keep the family rice plantation in McIntosh going for a decade after the war, paying former slaves to work the land. "Butler hired former slaves and paid them wages," Sullivan said. "They were fairly successful for a while."

But the coast's new economy was rooted firmly in the expansive acreage of pine forests to the west. Timber mills already were established on St. Simons Island and on the mainland near Brunswick, built by the Dart family whose ties to Glynn County date back to the Revolution. In the years after the war, Urbanus Dart sold the mills to New York businessman William E. Dodge, who also had purchased some 350,000 acres of towering Georgia pines forest stretching as far west as Macon.

Above the Altamaha River, McIntosh County native and former Confederate officer Joseph Hilton was op-

Brunswick promotional brochure, 1902

erating a burgeoning timber enterprise of his own. The Altamaha's flow from inland forests to the coast served as a natural delivery system of the much-sought-after Georgia pines. The felled pines were lashed together into great square rafts, then floated down to the coast.

Steam-powered towboats hauled lumber headed from the Altamaha to St. Simons Island and to Brunswick through a natural artery known as "3-mile cut," floating down on high tide. Hilton's timber mill sat along the bluff near the present site of the Fort King George State Historic site near Darien.

"The timber is cut (inland) within proximity to the Altamaha, because the river is the conveyor belt that gets the timber to the coast," Sullivan said. "Because of this, the region became very prosperous after the Civil War."

Tall-masted ships lined the docks at Sapelo Island and at the port on St. Simons Island at Gascoigne Bluff along the Frederica River. Of course, the present causeway was not even a dream back then, but Sullivan asked his audience to indulge their fancy.

Steamboat Hessie on its Brunswick-Darien run

"So if there had been a causeway coming over to St. Simons in 1885, and you looked over to the left coming across the bridge, this is what you would have seen — ships tied up loading lumber from St. Simons' mills. Even large oceangoing ships that came from Europe for Georgia pine. This was a huge operation."

The local timber industry stood even taller after 1888, when the Yankee Dodge and the ex-Confederate Hilton merged. In 1900, the Hilton-Dodge Lumber Company shipped some 112 million board feet of lumber out of the Georgia forests.

"When they merged, they became the largest timber company in the world," Sullivan said.

In addition to timber, those docks were stacked with barrels and barrels of turpentine and other pine resin products, known collectively as naval stores. The products could never shake that original term, applied back when pine sap was distilled almost entirely for sealants and caulking in marine construction. The turpentine trade brought an influx of newcomers from North Carolina, who were skilled at tapping pine sap.

"The ports of Brunswick and St. Simons became the worldwide leader of shipping naval stores," Sullivan said. "Thousands of barrels of turpentine would line the docks to be shipped around the world. And this all goes back to the ecology, because of the proximity of the Georgia pines and the river."

The timber and turpentine booms fueled an economy that brought transformations and advancements to the Golden Isles at a dizzying pace, especially by placid 19th Century standards. The once fledgling railroad systems gained ground, bringing Brunswick and its deepwater port into its own. The Brunswick and Western connected the port city with Albany; the Georgia Coastal and Piedmont led from Brunswick to Darien and northward to Ludowici. By extension, both systems connected the city to points beyond in both directions.

Brunswick's pre-war population was less than 1,000.

The Jekyll Island Club, 1890s

The city counted 9,000 residents during the 1870 census, Sullivan said. "The railroads made Brunswick sprout overnight," he said.

The St. Simons Pier was built at the site of the modern-day pier shortly after the Civil War, catering to visitors from the mainland who came over on the Emmeline or Hessie ferry boats for a day at the beach. More long-term guests could stay at the island's first hotel, built in 1883 near present-day Massengale Park, Sullivan said.

"St. Simons, even in the 1870s through the 1890s, was a very desirable place to come and visit," Sullivan said.

Not near so desirable, however, as neighboring Jekyll Island was to a group of movers and shakers from New York City. John Eugene duBignon, of the Jekyll Island plantation family, bought up the entire island in the years after the war. He subsequently sold it as the private playground of the wealthy elite.

Membership in the Jekyll Island Club included J.P. Morgan, William Rockefeller and Joseph Pulitzer. There on Jekyll they would while away the winter months from Christmas through Easter in luxury and mild Southern breezes. But don't expect Sullivan to scoff at the rich upper crust's indulgent lifestyles. These ruthless power brokers had a genuine soft spot for the Sea Islands, and they put their money where their hearts were. Along with Atlanta Coca Cola heir Asa Griggs Candler, these northern captains of finance outright bought six out of the eight coastal islands in Georgia.

"This to me was the first real conservation movement in Coastal Georgia," Sullivan said. "These were some of the wealthiest and most influential people of their time. They fell in love with the ecology and environment of our Georgia Coast, and they bought it so it could be preserved. That is why I have called them the first conservationists."

Part 6: Automobiles, men who made them shape 20th Century

For all their entrepreneurial vision, the great timber barons lacked foresight as the 20th century dawned on the Golden Isles and Coastal Georgia.

The seemingly unending stretch of virgin Georgia pine forest to the west proved to be finite after all — this despite the unprecedented 112 million board-feet of timber that was harvested in 1900. By 1910, a comparatively scant 16 million board feet of lumber trickled down the Altamaha River to the sawmills in Glynn and McIntosh counties. Poor stewardship ultimately busted the timber boom that had pulled the region out of the South's post-Civil War depression and helped fuel the 19th century's westward expansion.

But despite its people's short-sightedness in the realm of conservation, Coastal Georgia's natural resources just kept on giving. The saltwater that swirled around them from the marsh to the Atlantic saw to folks' needs during the first half of the 20th century, Coastal Georgia historian Buddy Sullivan said.

"Once again, everything is predicated on the ecology," Sullivan said.

Shipbuilding, commercial fishing and the growing oceanfront tourism trade put the wind in Coastal Georgia's sails during much of this period, Sullivan said. Roads cut through the landscape, while causeways and bridges spanned the waters, connecting the coastal communities like never before.

And perhaps the only thing that brought more change to Coastal Georgia than the automobile was the men who built them. Howard E. Coffin of the Hudson Motor Car Company

Howard E. Coffin

and Henry Ford both made homes on the Georgia Coast; both became benefactors to its people, black and white. They were among a second generation of American magnates who fell in love with the unique ecology and people of the region and invested heavily to protect both.

These wealthy transplants included Richard Joshua Reynolds Jr., the North Carolina tobacco heir who financed the birth of modern marine biology. Another was New York Yankees co-owner Col. T.L. Huston, whose dairy and vegetable farms on Butler Island put poor Coastal Georgians to work.

Coffin also created the luxury resort that today is Sea Island and built The Cloister hotel there. An Ohio native and an engineering graduate of the University of Michigan, Coffin "made valuable contributions to the early automobile industry," Sullivan said. Coffin bought Sapelo Island in McIntosh County in 1912, elaborately renovating the Spalding family's Sapelo House mansion, which had been ransacked by Yankees during the Civil War.

With his 124-foot yacht, Zapala, docked there, Coffin's Sapelo Island played host to the day's rich, influential and famous. Sitting President Calvin Coolidge was among his many prestigious visitors. Also dropping in on Sapelo was famed aviator Charles Lindbergh, who actually landed his plane on the island during a flight up the coast.

"Lindbergh landed in a cow field," Sullivan said.

Perhaps more revealing of his true nature was the respect Coffin extended to his neighbors, Sullivan said. Coffin had no intention of dispossessing Sapelo's fiercely-independent Geechee peoples, descendants of plantation slaves who learned to live as one with the land while maintaining a distinct culture and language.

Richard J. Reynolds, Jr.

"When he bought the island, he did not try to buy their land," Sullivan said. "He wanted them to keep their land, keep farming and living off of it. This is one of the ways he really showed his dedication to preserving the island."

Coffin, along with his young cousin Alfred W. Jones, had also acquired Glynn Isles, the small island on the ocean side of St. Simons. Jones renamed it Sea Island and the two began building one of the prime resort destinations of its day. Addison Mizner, the famed architect of Palm Beach mansions, was recruited in 1927 to build the resort island's crown jewel, The Cloister. The hotel was completed in 1928, a year before the Stock Market Crash.

Desperate for money to keep Sea Island afloat through the financial crisis, Coffin sold Sapelo to his friend and peer, R.J. Reynolds Jr. At $700,000, Reynolds drove a hard bargain and got the island for a song, even by 1934 standards. Coffin threw the Zapata in for an additional $50,000.

"Because of that sale, in about five years, Sea ▨ was able to turn a profit," Sullivan said.

After serving with distinction as a naval commander in the Pacific Theater during World War II, Reynolds became a proponent of marine research. In 1953, he financed the establishment of the 6,000-acre University of Georgia Marine Research Institute, where biology professor Eugene Odum became a leader in understanding the vital connections among neighboring ecosystems. "He was the father of modern ecology," Sullivan said of Odum. "Sapelo was pristine and isolated and they could really get into the understanding of how the marsh and the tides and marine life and shore birds and all of the rest of it interacted together. Nobody knew that before — that marshes, in essence, make that happen."

That same environment rejected the efforts of Henry Ford of the Ford Motor Company to establish a rubber plantation south of Savannah at Ways Station in 1925, later renamed Richmond Hill, Sullivan said.

Henry Ford Home in Richmond Hill

ees didn't grow very well here," he

, there was cabbage, lettuce and other
table crops. Ford grew them in large
his arrival in the 1920s, hiring local
ing and processing. And the town of
prouted up around his lavish Greek
on the Ogeechee River. Ford built pri-
mary schools for blacks in the area. Despite his wealth,
Ford was known to mingle with workers in the fields,
Sullivan said.

"There are still people in Richmond Hill who speak
lovingly of him as Mr. Ford," he said. "He brought
progress to that area of the Georgia Coast where before
it was impoverished."

Automobile ownership was an early indication of a
family's rise out of poverty in those days, this once luxury acquisition made possible to the masses by Ford's
production innovations. In 1920, an early stretch of
present-day U.S. Highway 17 was completed, connecting Brunswick with Darien by roadway for the first
time. An even bigger game-changer was the causeway
connecting Brunswick and St. Simons Island, a byway
completed in 1924 under the direction of homegrown
engineer F.J. Torras.

"By 1924 you could go to St. Simons by car, and this
changed the whole dynamic of the island," Sullivan
said. "Where before it was mostly a sawmill community
and thinly populated, afterward you see it become an
even more thriving tourism destination."

Tourism, automobile joyrides and most all other
light-hearted pursuits reeled to a halt in December
of 1941, when the Japanese bombing of Pearl Harbor
brought America into World War II. With its deep
water port, Brunswick quickly galvanized itself as a

Brunswick shipyard built 99 Liberty Ships

valued contributor to the war effort. A six-slip shipyard emerged on the Brunswick River, producing 99 Liberty Ships from 1943-45.

Naval Air Station Glynco went up at the site of present day Brunswick Golden Isles Airport, housing the huge lighter-than-air blimps that escorted merchant ships and patrolled the coast for German U-boats. And the threat was real.

War came to the home front on April 8, 1942, when a U-boat torpedoed and sank the tankers Esso Baton Rouge and S.S. Oklahoma, killing 22 crewmen. "This gives you an idea of the immediacy of the war right here," he said.

Folks driving south over the Sidney Lanier Bridge today can see the remains of the slips on which the completed Liberty Ships were launched into the Brunswick River. Delivering men, arms and equipment to the warfront, the liberty ships proved vital to the war effort. So too were the men and women back home who built them, cranking out the ships at a rate that outpaced enemy efforts to destroy them.

Blimps at Glynco naval Base near Brunswick

"The population of Brunswick just exploded over the war years with workers coming to work on the Liberty Ships," he said. "You can see how valuable this area was to the overall war effort."

With the nation returning to a festive mood at war's end, a more familiar ship returned to waters off of the golden isles to help feed the celebration. The locally-iconic shrimp trawlers filled the offshore seascape in record numbers in the late 1940s through the 1960s, heralded as the "gold rush" days of the Georgia shrimp harvest.

The so-called "blue water" boats of this era were bigger, better built and included technology such as on-board ice machines that allowed crews to stay out longer and catch more shrimp.

"This was considered the Seafood Capital of the World at one time, and it was not much of an exaggeration," Sullivan said. "There were seafood processing plants on St. Simons and in Brunswick. You could go down to the docks in Brunswick and all along it would literally be crawling with boats."

Shrimping as an industry in the Golden Isles has it beginnings in the 1920s, influenced heavily by Portuguese immigrants of proud seafaring stock who settled along our coast to ply their trade.

That shrimping tradition survives today, like so many other treasured legacies from the rich and storied history of Coastal Georgia.

"It's important to remember that this is all part of our heritage," said Sullivan, whose dad briefly engaged in shrimping and oystering after World War II. "They came before us, but they make us who we are. The Georgia Coast is pristine, it's beautiful and it's natural."

With Buddy, it always come back to this: the salt marsh and the rivers, and the natural bounty that presides where the land meets the sea. And that is where it all started — about 25,000 years ago at the tail end of the last Ice Age, the one scientists call the Pleistocene.

~7: Women were often Coastal History's makers, caretakers

The Golden Isles has a complex and multi-faceted history, one that would be incomplete without also including her story.

From a captivating Native American trader to a meticulous and empathetic plantation manager, through the centuries the story of Coastal Georgia is often writ large with a decidedly feminine touch. They not only wove themselves into the fabric of the region's history, women most often were its caretakers — dutifully recording it for posterity, Sullivan notes.

In the early days of Colonial settlement on the Georgia Coast, chances were favorable that trade goods needed by settlers from here to the Carolinas first went through the hands of Mary Musgrove. Born around 1700 to a Creek mother and the English trader Edward Griffin, Musgrove combined entrepreneurial savvy with a keen understanding of both cultures to foster her own business ambitions while serving as a peaceful link between colonists and Native Americans. Artist renderings of this shrewd businesswoman often favor her with romance novel paperback cover features — flowing raven hair, fiery eyes and high native cheekbones.

"She was said to be an attractive woman," Sullivan said.

Painting of Mary Musgrove

Mary Musgrove grew up in both worlds. She spoke English and the native Muskogee language fluently. She was recognized as a full member of the Creek tribe and openly accepted in white society, thus gaining the trust of both peoples. She married English trader John Musgrove in 1717 and together they established a vital trading post on the Savannah River.

As an interpreter and an astute observer of the motives of both Creek Indians and English settlers, Musgrove became a leader in the deerskin trade from Georgia to the Carolinas. After John Musgrove's death in 1735, Mary Musgrove relocated the trading post farther up the Savannah River, to Yamacraw Bluff.

With Georgia's establishment as a British Colony in 1733, colony founder James Oglethorpe depended heavily on Mary Musgrove as an interpreter and liaison between the Creek and their new European neighbors. Her mediation of early communications between Oglethorpe and Yamacraw Chief Tomochichi helped lay the groundwork for the peaceful founding of the city of Savannah. Musgrove profited both in wealth and reputation as Oglethorpe's primary interpreter from 1733 to '43.

She would marry twice more and establish yet another trading post, this one farther south on the Altamaha River.

She and her third husband, the Rev. Thomas Bosomworth, became embroiled in a heated dispute with the British government when they sought to claim Ossabaw, Sapelo and St. Catherine's islands, pledged to them as a gift from Lower Creek Chief Malatchi. In a compromise, the British later granted them possession of St. Catherine's Island. There Mary spent her final days, dying in 1763.

"She became known as one of the leading traders," Sullivan said. "She was crucial to Oglethorpe's success, as she was the chief liaison between the British and the Indians. We don't always hear about her contributions in the early days, but she was very significant to establishing the trade routes."

By the next century the frontier environment of Mary Musgrove's Coastal Georgia had given way to the Antebellum-era of sprawling plantations. While the heady wealth of agricultural commerce was most decidedly a men's club, nobody operated a plantation more efficiently and effectively than Anna Page King.

During her time as its chief administrator, Retreat Plantation on St. Simons Island thrived on Sea Island cotton, while also cultivating fruit and citrus orchards and tropical gardens on more than 2,000 acres. Anna's husband, Thomas Butler King, contributed little, if any at all, to the operation of Retreat Plantation. A Massachusetts native, King was a politician and something of a speculator who spent little actual time at Retreat.

While Anna's correspondence reveals a longing for her husband to spend more time at home, she hardly needed

Ruins of Retreat plantation on St. Simon's Island

his help running a plantation.

Born in 1798, she grew up at Retreat as the daughter of William Page. William Page bought the estate in 1804 from Thomas Spalding. And on that plantation, he raised Anna Matilda Page to break the proverbial glass ceilings of 19th Century America.

Under his tutelage, Anna was groomed to tend to the myriad responsibilities of managing a plantation. That she learned these lessons well is detailed in "Letters of a St. Simons Island Plantation Mistress," a book that emerged from her journals on the day-to-day life of Retreat Plantation.

Her record keeping was meticulous and exact. She was considered humane for a slaveholder, and those under bondage on Retreat Plantation were treated with comparative care and compassion. Retreat even operated a slave hospital. Anna delegated much of the responsibility for treatment to slaves to Sukey and Mily, a mother and her daughter who were trained as nurses and midwives.

Anna's precise and detailed records of the life at Retreat provide historians with one of the more accurate depictions of life on an antebellum plantation, Sullivan said. She died in 1859, five years prior to the start of the Civil War and the end of the Antebellum South.

"This is one of the rare instances where a woman in those days was operating and managing a plantation, and doing it better than most," he said.

Anna Page King's example of accurately documenting history was followed by still more women in succeeding generations. Prominent among them were Lydia Parrish and Margaret Davis Cate.

Parrish's compilation of oral histories and photographs of African American slave descendants along the Georgia Coast were published in the 1930's and 40's. In particular her book, Slave Songs of the Golden Isles, provided one of the most unique and thorough depictions of their unique traditions and way of life up to that time.

"It's a fascinating account," Sullivan said. "She came to St. Simons and Sapelo islands and compiled their stories, documenting their traditions and the deep ties to their African roots."

A native of Glynn County, Margaret Davis Cate became one of the first local investigative historians, conducting painstaking records research through the first half of the 20th Century. Her work, including the books, Our Todays and Yesterdays and Early Days of Coastal Georgia, provided a foundation for the accurate documentation of the local historical landscape, Sullivan said.

"She was the pioneer of our local history," Sullivan said. "She was the first person to really get into the Glynn County Courthouse and look at the records and detail the history it revealed. Her work really laid the groundwork for our comprehensive history."

Part 8: Black history is a Tale of Fortitude and Perseverance

The slave called Neptune was bound to the Kings of Retreat Plantation on St. Simons Island. But it was a lifetime of enduring friendship, not bondage, which spurred Neptune to retrieve Henry Lord King's body from the carnage of a Civil War battlefield.

Today, the man and his unconditional act of love serve as the namesake for Neptune Park. The sprawling oceanfront green beside the Pier Village on St. Simons Island serves as a place where, among a rainbow of other cultures, both the descendants of slaves and of slave holders now gather in fellowship and harmony.

Farther north on St. Simons Island is Ebo Landing, a lesser known but more striking testament to the harsh legacy of slavery. It is said that here on Dunbar Creek numerous members of the Igbo tribe, newly-arrived from Africa, drowned themselves en masse rather than endure a life of slavery.

From Neptune's heartfelt act of devotion to the Igbos' resolve to live free or die, the story of African Americans on the Georgia Coast is one of perseverance, fortitude and of the inextinguishable spark within the human spirit. Examples of both Neptune and the Igbo inform the proud traditions of the Geechee. These Coastal Georgia people kindled their African customs in a new land despite centuries of enslavement. The Geechee value their independence just as they honor their allegiances to place and people.

Geechee culture fairly mirrors that of the South Carolinian

Born a slave on St. Simons, Neptune Small would die an Island landowner

Gullahs, but an outsider should not try to bandy the
about, Sullivan said.

"Gullah is South Carolina — Geechee is Georgia
"They're very defensive about that. And then the.
water Geechee — descendants of island cotton plantati.
the freshwater Geechee, who came from rice plantations."

Some historians say that the term Geechee may be derivative
from the Ogeechee River near Savannah where bondsmen were
first brought from South Carolina when slavery was legalized in
the Georgia colony. Like their Gullah kin, the Geechee are unique
in the sad tale of slavery in America, because human and geographical circumstances afforded them a certain degree of independence scarcely seen among slaves elsewhere.

The agricultural technology and irrigation practices employed
on Coastal Georgia rice plantations were of African origin, as
noted in Chapter 3 of this book. When it came to planting and
harvesting, most knew the process involved better than the
whites who profited from it. And the Africans themselves were
better acclimated than the white Europeans to the malarial conditions that prevailed in the region.

In fact, Thomas Spalding assigned the slave Bilali Mohammad
as overseer of his Sapelo Island cotton plantation. Many of Bilali's proud descendants live among us on the Georgia Coast still
today.

When the freedom of emancipation came after the Civil War,
the Geechee attained independence in the most literal sense.
Melding their African ancestry with new traditions, the Geechee
developed a distinct dialect, musical tradition and culture. After
generations of immersion in the local environment and the rich-
es of its natural resources, they were able to settle in and among
the barrier islands without much need of outside assistance or
influence.

"Their culture and its African roots are well-documented,"
Sullivan said, noting the enclave of Geechee who still live in
isolated Sapelo Island's Hog Hammock community. "These
were very hardy, very independent people, who loved their

Art by LaRue, Dee Williams

self-sufficiency."

Such traits coursed through the veins of the indomitable Igbo, a tribe who hailed from the West African region of present day Nigeria. Indeed, the Igbo (sometimes referred to as Ebo) had gained a reputation throughout the slave-holding South for being virulently resistant to attempts at subjugation.

The story of Ebo landing begins in Savannah, with the arrival directly from Africa of slaves from that tribe. They were sold in 1803 at auction in Savannah, acquired for the St. Simons Island plantations of John Couper and Thomas Spalding.

They arrived at Dunbar Creek on St. Simons Island aboard the small sailing ship Morovia. Part legend and part fact, versions of the journey vary. By one account, the Igbo rebelled against the ship's crewmen, who were either thrown or jumped overboard to their deaths. Such a rebellion is not mentioned in other historical accounts.

Upon arriving at Dunbar Creek, the Igbo did go into the water, however. A white man who witnessed the macabre scene said the

Igbo "took to the swamp" and drowned rather than face a life in chains.

Generations of African American oral history speak of the defiant act as one of reverent salvation, not of death. In fact, Igbo spiritual tradition holds that they simply went home, returning by the ocean from whence they came.

Skeptics speculate that the Igbo drownings were accidental and a result panic rather than the ultimate act of willful resistance.

Sullivan does not sound like a skeptic.

"They were brought directly from West Africa," Sullivan said. "Some or all of them, rather than submit to slavery, walked into the river and drowned. There is some strong validity to that story."

Unlike the Igbo, Neptune was born into slavery, the child of slaves.

The son of Sukey, a head nurse at Retreat's hospital for slaves, Neptune was chosen at birth to be a playmate for the six King sons. He was born just a few months after Henry Lord King, and the two quickly formed a lasting bond. It is said that plantation matriarch Ann Page King taught Neptune to read and write along with her son Lordy.

He had a privileged life as far as slaves go. Neptune was a slave nonetheless. So when Lord King went off to serve as an officer in the Confederacy during the Civil War, Neptune too went off to war, as a manservant to his childhood friend.

The Battle of Fredericksburg (Va.) was a great victory for Confederate Gen. Robert E. Lee, but it was a tragedy for the King family. Lord King had volunteered to carry a message across dangerous territory to another sector of the Confederate lines.

When he did not return by sundown, Neptune ventured into the bloody no-man's land between the battle lines and found his beloved friend's body in the dark among the scores of dead and dying. Neptune then began the journey to bring King's body home to his family, delivering his friend's body first to Savannah. At war's end, Lord was buried in the family plot at Christ Church on St. Simons Island.

Neptune adopted the last name Small upon gaining freedom, apparently a self-appraisal of his physical stature. He also became a landowner, a gift of gratitude from the King family for bringing Lord home.

"They were so grateful for that gesture that they gave him property from their lands," Sullivan said. "It's really one of the nice stories that comes from St. Simons during that era. And there is ample documentation to support it."

Buddy's suggested reading list

If this little manuscript has inspired you to delve deeper into the fascinating history of Coastal Georgia, here is Buddy's suggested reading list. This list is included in the handout package that each participant receives at the start of Buddy's lecture series. It also represents some of the numerous books he has read during research on the 25 books he has authored. Enjoy.

SELECTED BOOKS ABOUT COASTAL GEORGIA HISTORY & CULTURE

Bailey, Cornelia, God, Dr. Buzzard and the Bolito Man (Sapelo Geechee life and culture)

Bailey, Eloise, Camden's Challenge (history of Camden County and St. Marys)

Bartram, William, Travels, Naturalist Edition (Useful to understanding natural history of coast)

Bell, Malcolm, Major Butler's Legacy, Five Generations of a Slave-holding Family (definitive)

Bragg, William Harris, De Renne: Three Generations of a Georgia Family (Savannah, definitive)

Bullard, Mary R., Cumberland Island: A History (outstanding history of the island).

Cate, Margaret Davis, Our Todays and Yesterdays (dated, but thorough, Glynn County history)

Clarke, Erskine, Dwelling Place (From the slaves' perspective at Jones plantation, Liberty Co.)

Coulter, Ellis M., Thomas Spalding of Sapelo (dated, but only biography of Spalding).

Coulter, Ellis M., ed., Georgia's Disputed Ruins (1930s tabby controversy, a classic)

Couper, Caroline Lovell, The Golden Isles of Georgia (1932. A somewhat romanticized history)

Davis, Jingle, Island Time (outstanding account of St. Simons Island history and culture)

Davis, Jingle, Island Passages (Jekyll Island, companion volume to above)

Duncan, Russell, Freedom's Shore: Tunis Campbell and the Georgia Freedmen

Fendig, Bruce, Brunswick: Ocean Port of Georgia (vintage photographs of town, 1870-1950)

Ferguson, Reed, The John Couper Family of Cannon's Point (antebellum St. Simons Island)

Fraser, Walter J., Lowcountry Hurricanes (scholarly review of Georgia hurricanes).

Georgia Writers Project, Drums and Shadows, Survival Studies Among the Georgia Coastal Negroes (reprint of classic 1940 account of black culture on the sea islands)

Granger, Mary, ed., Savannah River Plantations (definitive account of Savannah rice planters)

Greene, Melissa F., Praying for Sheetrock (prize winning account of civil rights in Darien area)

Hoffman, Paul, A New Andalucia and a Way to the Orient (Spanish exploration of the coast)

Ivers, Larry, British Drums on the Southern Frontier (Oglethorpe and the War with Spain)

Jones, C. C., The Dead Towns of Georgia (1878. The coast's "lost" towns, including Frederica)

Keber, Martha, Seas of Gold, Seas of Cotton (Christophe Dubignon and Jekyll Island)

Kemble, Frances Anne, Journal of a Residence on a Georgian Plantation in 1838-1839

Kimsey & Kinard, eds., Marshes of Glynn: World War II (oral history memoirs of the homefront)

Lane, Mills B., ed., General Oglethorpe's Georgia: Colonial Letters, 1733-1743 (outstanding)

Lawrence, Alexander A., Storm Over Savannah (Savannah during the Revolution)

Lawrence, Alexander A., A Present for Mr. Lincoln (Savannah during the Civil War)

Leigh, Frances Butler, Ten Years on a Georgia Plantation Since the War (Reconstruction)

Lindsay, Melanie, ed., Anna: Letters of a St. Simons Island Plantation Mistress, 1817-1859

June Hall, The Jekyll Island Club, Southern Haven for Mil-
efinitive account)

n, June Hall, Jekyll Island's Early Years (colonial, antebellum
War)

n, Harold, This Happy Isle (Very readable account of Sea Island
and the Cloister)

Myers, Robert M., ed., The Children of Pride (Liberty County Jones
family letters, 1854-1868)

Reynolds and Schactman, The Gilded Leaf (R.J. Reynolds family with
much about Sapelo)

Russell, Preston, Savannah: The History of Her People (best overview
of Savannah history)

Seabrook, Charles, The World of the Salt Marsh (good ecological sur-
vey of the Georgia coast)

Smith, Julia F., Slavery and Rice Culture in Lowcountry Georgia (definitive account of subject)

Stewart, Mart, What Natures Suffers to Groe (tidewater agricultural and
economic history)

Sullivan, Buddy, Sapelo: People and Place on a Georgia Sea Island

→ Sullivan, Buddy, Early Days on the Georgia Tidewater (primarily
Darien and Sapelo history)

Sullivan, Buddy, All Under Bank (antebellum Butler Island and Liberty
County plantations).

→ Sullivan, Buddy, High Water on the Bar, (postbellum lumber industry,
Darien & St Simons

Vanstory, Burnette, Georgia's Land of the Golden Isles (excellent overview, emphasis on SSI)

Thomas, David H., St. Catherines: An Island in Time (archaeology of
Mission Santa Catalina)

Wood, Virginia S., Live Oaking, Southern Timber for Tall Ships (definitive, includes St. Simons)

Worth, John E., The Struggle for the Georgia Coast (definitive account
of the Spanish missions)